C000212155

A BOOT UP

THE BERKSHIRE DOWNS

Robert Wood

First published in Great Britain in 2010

British Library Cataloguing-in-Publication Data
A CIP record for this title is available from the British Library

ISBN 978 1 906887 71 1

PiXZ Books
Halsgrove House, Ryelands Industrial Estate,
Bagley Road, Wellington, Somerset TA21 9PZ
Tel: 01823 653777
Fax: 01823 216796
email: sales@halsgrove.com

An imprint of Halstar Ltd, part of the Halsgrove group of companies
Information on all Halsgrove titles is available at: www.halsgrove.com

Printed and bound by Toppan Leefung Printers Ltd, China

Contents

About this book and how to use it

The Area

The Berkshire Downs are a line of downland hills, part of the North Wessex Area of Outstanding Natural Beauty. They have attracted human habitation since prehistoric times. Geologically they are continuous with the Marlborough Downs to the west and the Chilterns to the east. They lie east-west, with their scarp slope facing north into the Vale of the White Horse and their dip slope bounded by the course of the River Kennet. In the east they are divided from the Chilterns by the River Thames. Downland pasture is firm and well-drained, suited to grazing sheep and training horses. Horse racing is a major business in the area. Gallops are everywhere. Can downland be cultivated? There are at least three Starveall Farms in the area and with 'starveall' meaning 'poor land' it might be thought that the thin chalky downland soil has defeated farmers but the evidence seems to suggest otherwise.

These walks cover more or less the length of the Berkshire Downs, from Ashdown House in the west to the National Trust properties – Lardon Chase, Lough Down and the Holies – in the east. The Ridgeway, the spine of the Downs, is never far away. Some walks stray into Oxfordshire but that is understandable; until 1974 an area like Moulsford lay in Berkshire. Historical and literary associations are everywhere, from a battle fought by King Alfred (then a prince), possible complicity by a Catholic grandee in the Gunpowder Plot, two monuments to soldiers one very grand, the ubiquitous John Betjeman, a once-famous sheep fair, through to *Wind in the Willows, Three Men in a Boat, Worzel Gummidge* and Thomas Hardy's last novel *Jude the Obscure*.

The Routes

All routes are circular. They vary from 3½ to 8½ miles and are graded from one to three boots – from easy to more challenging. Routes are along public rights of way or occasionally unmarked but sanctioned tracks or across open access land. Please remember that conditions under foot will vary greatly according to the season and the weather. Other than that all seasons have something going for them depending on taste; for this writer it is bluebells in the spring, sun to shade in summer, sloes and blackberries in autumn and clear blue skies in winter.

This book is no different from others in assuming that the great majority of walkers will arrive by car. Public transport can be used in principle but, depending on the journey to be undertaken, at least one change is liable to be required e.g. a journey from Newbury to Blewbury.

The countryside is never free of danger but the greatest risk comes crossing roads. Likely danger spots are flagged up. The A338 and the A417 need extra vigilance.

The Maps

Though a self-contained potted description of each walk is provided a map is needed to locate the starts. The sketch maps can only be a rough guide. Three Ordnance Survey maps currently cover the entire Berkshire Downs – Explorer 158, 159 and 170, of which 170 is easily the most heavily used.

Looking over Blewbury

View across to Lambourn church

Key to Symbols Used

Level of difficulty:
Easy
Moderate
More Challenging

Map symbols:

🚗	Park & start
	Tarred Road
---	Footpath
	River, stream or brook
■	Building
+	Church
▲	Triangulation pillar or other landmark
🍺	Pub

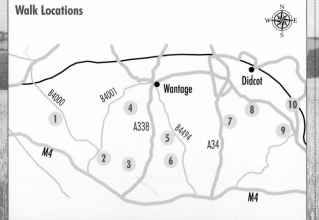

Walk Locations

B4000
B4001
• Wantage
• Didcot
A338
B4494
A34
M4
M4

1 2 3 4 5 6 7 8 9 10

1 Ashdown House

A 5-mile circuit round and about a superb mansion with a tale to tell

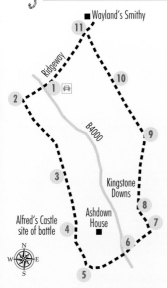

Level: 🥾🥾
Length: 5 miles
Terrain: One downhill section, one steepish scramble; one slightly uphill stretch to regain the Ridgeway
Park and start: The car park at the junction of the Ridgeway with the B4001 (GR 273843)
Map: OS Explorer 170
Websites: www.nationaltrust.org.uk/main/w-vh/w-visits/w-findaplace/w-ashdownhouse
www.victorianweb.org/art/illustration/doyle/2

Starting on the Ridgeway this walk curls round Ashdown House, a splendid 17th century property set in a remote downland location, before heading back up to the higher ground and the Ridgeway. It is said that in 1662 the first Earl of Craven was fleeing the plague in London on a lone stallion, when he arrived, exhausted, at his little-frequented Berkshire estates. The Earl decided to build himself a house as a country refuge for his love, the Queen of Bohemia, sister of King Charles I, known as 'The Winter Queen'. Construction began soon afterward but, unfortunately, the lady died that same year. Such a romantic story. Built in the tall Dutch gabled style the house remains ravishing to the eye. Incidentally, Ashdown is reckoned to be an ancient name for the whole of the Berkshire Downs.

Alfred's Castle

The age of the Ridgeway is uncertain. Best estimates date it to the Bronze Age some 3,000 years ago. In the middle ages the track was used by drovers to bring cattle and sheep from the West Country and Wales to the London market. To accommodate the livestock the hedges had to be at least 30 feet apart. The track is not so wide here, much wider elsewhere. Following the introduction of turnpikes in the 18th century, the drovers continued to use the track to avoid tolls, until the advent of railways.

1 Set off west along the Ridgeway perhaps thinking of all those who have wandered along this track ("And did those feet in ancient times").

2 Before long a crossing of tracks comes up. Blank out the sign to the pub on the right and go left along the edge of a bean field. At the first patch of wood to the left look for a little stile. Once over it continue southwards through a green space keeping the wood to the left and the edge of the field to the right.

3 Go over another a stile in the middle of the field and head for the far right corner. The rocky feature over the fence is an Iron Age hill fort.

Ashdown House avenue

It was on this lump of rock that King Alfred, then a prince of 21, led a force of 800 to 1000 West Saxons to victory over the Danes. The date was 8 January 871. But the great loss of life on both sides rendered Alfred's success somewhat bitter-sweet and on receiving reinforcements the Danes were able subsequently to win several victories.

4 Go over the stile and proceed downhill, perhaps pausing to imagine the battle. A real treat is coming up in a moment so be prepared to be bowled over. There it is: over to the left, through the trees, is Ashdown House.

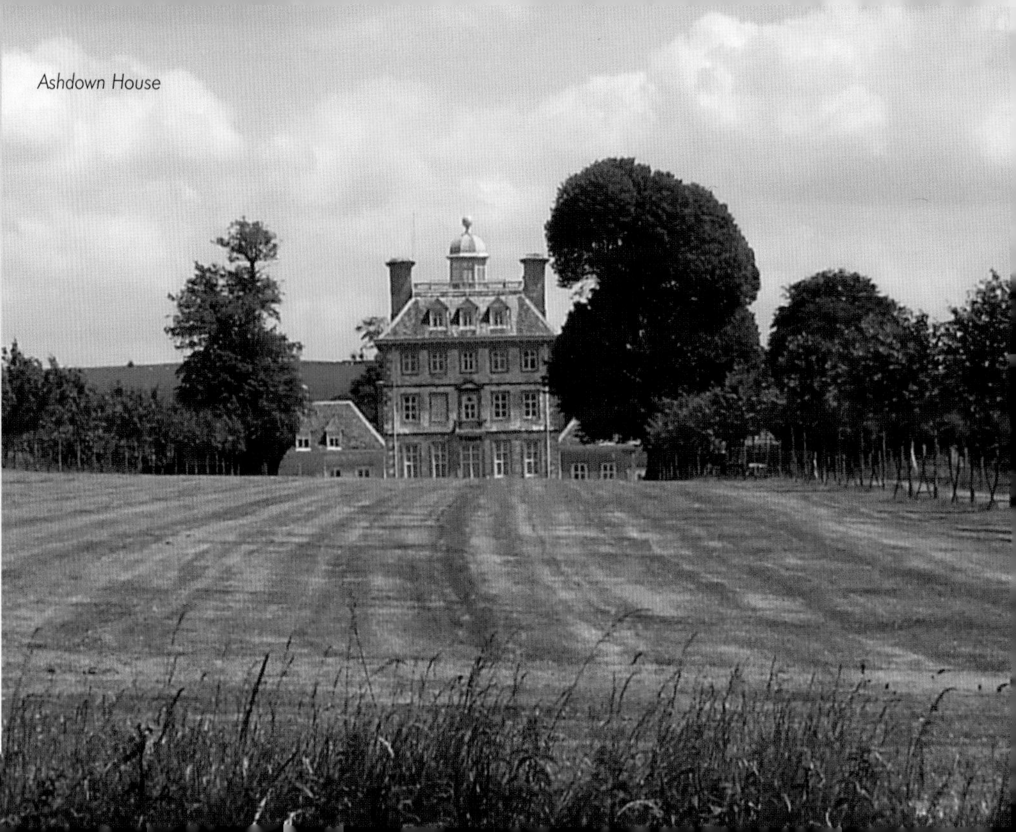

Ashdown House

5 At the bottom of the incline is a track that leads left onto a lane. Walk along the lane admiring the National Trust Estate barn to the right. Then, on the left, behind its tall gates, is the house again, looking if possible even more splendid.

6 Continue along the lane to the B4000. Opposite stands an NT sign and a display board. Two tracks lead over the hill. The left is preferred but it is not obvious where it goes. However, there is a path visible towards the top of the hill. Take it; it will make no difference at the top.

7 Once at the top, spot a weathercock ahead. Pay it a visit by all means but be aware that the next stage starts at the signpost

that is sited diagonally left uphill (GR 287825). How the signpost is reached does not matter because this is open access land. En route to the signpost look back towards Ashdown House and marvel at the sight.

8 Take the clearly demarcated path through a field. At a very rusty signpost press on all the while admiring the downland scenery over to the right.

A megalithic chambered tomb built about 3400 BC; Wayland's Smithy is associated with Wayland the Norse and Saxon god of blacksmithing. According to legend, a traveller whose horse had lost a shoe could leave the animal and a silver coin there overnight and next morning the horse would be re-shod. Just like that!

9 At the next junction take the bridleway to the left and proceed up a slight incline towards a gap in a stand of trees off in the distance.

10 Once through the gap continue along a pleasant avenue flanked by hawthorn bushes. When a barn comes up on the left the Ridgeway is very close.

11 Once at the Ridgeway turn left unless a visit to Wayland's Smithy beckons. This atmospheric feature is a little way down on the right. Otherwise, and in any case, the car is but a short distance to the west.

Ridgeway signpost

2 **Lambourn Woodlands**

A 4-mile saunter full of interest

This walk is as good a way of spending a couple of hours as any. A medieval village, Second World War tragedies, a Roman road, a 17th century mansion, a habitat of rare butterflies: they are all here. Enjoy.

Level: ♥ ♥

Length: 4¼ miles

Terrain: Variable; two flat stretches; four ups and four downs but nothing too steep.

Park and start: On the eastern side of Lambourn village outside a derelict pub. *The Lamb* at the junction of Newbury Road and Mill Lane (GR 330787).

Map: OS Explorer 158

Websites: www.berkshirehistory.com/villages/lambourn_woodlands
www.ramsburyatwar.com/crashsites

Rooksnest garden

Lambourn Woodlands

On Thorn Hill

1 Notice the River Lambourn as it meanders pleasantly past the side of the pub. Cross over Newbury Road to a signpost by the side of the fire station. At a crossing of the ways, go left to join the Lambourn Valley Way, which features at the start of the Sheepdrove walk.

2 Proceed through a gate to emerge onto a recreation ground. Cross to the corner where there is tarmac for parking. Take care crossing the little stile. After a short section of field another stile comes up. Go left and continue until the road bears left taking the Lambourn Valley Way with it.

3 Pass through a gate beside an electricity sub-station and follow a track through some grass. Go through another gate and continue across a meadow. To the left is Bockhampton Manor (said to date from Tudor times, although it is principally William and Mary) with its grass tennis court, not so often seen.

4 Go through a gate beside a pumping station and turn right up a fine broad track (Thorn Hill). Look behind and to the left to see what the Sheepdrove walk has in store.

Rooksnest

Dating from the 17th century, 'Rooksnest' has a fine garden that is open periodically under the National Gardens Scheme.

5 At the top of the hill bear right to skirt some woodland. Continue over a crossing of the ways and through some pleasant shady woodland before reaching another crossing of the ways where once again the route lies ahead.

6 A little way up the track look out for a stile to the left and a sign advertising a small pond on the other side. Why not hop over and take a look? At the top of the incline a sign announces the Rooksnest estate. Very soon the house and gardens come up on the left.

7 Follow the road past the house to a junction. While the way ahead is to the right, Ermin Street is just to the left; Ermin Street, the Roman road that ran between Silchester and Cirencester. Having turned right, emerge very soon into a fine open space. Over to the left in the corner of the field is an old thatched cottage. And this field? It was once — believe it or not — an airfield in the Second World War; Membury airfield. It seems so minute.

8 Dance's Cottage is pure Hansel and Gretel; the walls must have some tales to tell. Bear right round the edge of some woodland before ducking into a wood. This is Gifford Copse, the scene of a crash during WW2. Go down through the wood, taking care because the track can be muddy. At the bottom go right for a short distance to a signpost. The crash occurred off to the right.

9 Go uphill and then down again onto a short flat

On 25th April 1944, shortly after takeoff from Membury, a C-47 Skytrain crashed killing all 14 onboard. It was a bad year for the US forces at Membury. On 19th September, at Strouds Farm, just across Ermin Street from Rooksnest, two gliders collided; all eight occupants dying instantly. The official crash report concluded that 'carelessness on the part of one or other (of the pilots) caused the crash'. It seems that the pilots were involved in a drunken quarrel before the flight – enough said.

section. Over to the left is Boldstart Farm, like many downland farms situated so as to obtain maximum

shelter from the elements. Now climb the hill and at the crest enjoy another superb view of the Lambourn Downs.

White Shute, over to the right, is a Site of Special Scientific Interest (SSSI). It is an important habitat for butterflies and caterpillars, some rare.

Dance's Cottage

17

10 Some way downhill a track comes in on the right. This spot is called Hungerford Gap although it is not clear why. Perhaps it was a gap off what is clearly the major trail over White Shute which travellers specifically wanting Hungerford would have needed to nip through.

11 Proceed more or less straight ahead past a wooden structure.

View across to Lambourn church

The space to the right and down to the river was once occupied by a medieval village.

12 To exit the field aim for a corrugated iron roof over in the left corner. Pass to the left of it onto the road encountered at the start. From here go back through the field, over the tricky stile, and across the recreation ground before turning right to regain Newbury Road and the car.

The land surrounding the village was enclosed as parkland – "emparked" – by the Lord of Bockhampton Manor, so in effect the villagers were locked out. This particular Lord had to perform an unusual service to the King in order to retain his Manor. Where other Lords had to provide fighting men or cash in kind, Bockhampton had to provide a medieval joke. The text literally translates that he had to perform a hop, a skip and, well, something rude …

Thanks to Roger Day for help with the crash material.

3 In Sheepdrove Country

3 In Sheepdrove Country

Invigorating 7-mile circuit through definitive downland scenery

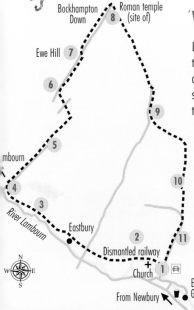

Bockhampton Down
Roman temple (site of)
8
Ewe Hill 7
6
9
5
mbourn
4
10
3
River Lambourn
Eastbury
2
11
Dismantled railway
Church
East Garston
From Newbury

'Valley of the Racehorse' say the signs on approaching the large village of Lambourn. A railway once ran along this valley but it never made money and was finally closed in 1973. It is said that the locals preferred to tell the time by the trains rather than to travel on them. The walk follows a section of the old track bed westwards almost into Lambourn before heading up to the downs. Everywhere gallops are evident but to see galloping it is best to go first thing.

Level: 🦋🦋
Length: 7½ miles
Terrain: Variable; flat to start with, then up to the downs followed by a short level stretch and a sequence of rises and falls, but nothing too steep.

Park and start: East Garston village is just off the Newbury-Lambourn road. Drive westwards through the village towards the church. Within sight of the church look for a little road off to the right – called 'Downlands' – and park in the space at the end (GR 363769).

Maps: OS Explorer 158 and 170
Website: www.subbrit.org.uk/sb sites/stations/e/east_garston/index

Above Lambourn

1 Go through a gap in the hedge and turn right. Just before the church drive there are footpath signs signalling the Lambourn Valley Way. Here is where the railway went through East Garston — the station was up on the right. Go left, keeping the church to your right.

2 The path does not stick slavishly to the railway bed and before long there is a kink in the path where the two part company. Climb the steps and at the top turn right, continue along the edge of the field before turning right and then left to re-join the railway bed. The path skirts the next village — Eastbury — where there was a station, no longer evident. Before long a proper piece of railway furniture materialises. Surely those are level crossing gates! And spot the rusty spanner sitting on top of one of the posts (GR 342777).

3 Over the next stile is a field. The exact line of the path is not entirely obvious; best to aim to the right of the house ahead. Very soon what was once Bockhampton Halt comes up. It was here that the railway crossed the road. It seems that the crossing gates were normally kept locked so that a junior member of staff had to be sent from Lambourn on the station bicycle in time for every train — shades of *Oh! Mr Porter*.

(4) Start ascending the little road. Quite soon a little path between trees opens up to the left, not signposted but useful for getting off the road and also offering fine views of Lambourn down below.

(5) Soon the road becomes a track called Long Hedge. Continue until an impasse forces a left turn. Again there are fine views, both ahead and to the right; more gallops too. Negotiate the next stretch, which may be boggy, to reach Eastbury Down.

Horses of course

(6) Cross the first road and at the next go right passing first Hyde Farm to the left and then, some way along on the right, College Farm. By now it will have dawned that this is Sheepdrove country, with its Eco Conference Centre somewhere ahead of you.

(7) Look out for a display board planted by a gate and a stile. Among other things it invites the walker to enjoy the springy turf of Bockhampton Down. Accept the invitation – for this is a beautiful spot – and proceed in a more or less parallel fashion to the road before emerging at a red-roofed barn. Perhaps the Roman settlers felt the beauty of this place too because they built a temple at the junction up ahead, also a burial site, but there is nothing to be seen now.

(8) Leaving the red-roofed barn behind follow an obvious track downhill for the best part of a mile. Expect red kites and buzzards for company. At an obvious junction go ahead before, at a signpost, veering

It is said that Lambourn was named after the lambs that were dipped in the local river. Training gallops on the downs were begun in the 1760s by the Duke of Cumberland who must have realised that the well-drained and springy downland turf is perfect for the conditioning of race horses (the Duke could not have imagined that the horses would get baths).

over to the left to join a grassy path that will run parallel to the road before merging with it further on.

9 At a signpost take the path indicated, going uphill rather than straight. Ignore the signpost to the right and continue to the top where there is a choice — walk southwards along the rim of the field

Sheepdrove Organic Farm was established in 1997. It has earned a series of awards over the years. The Eco Conference Centre can be hired for events although a 'green' theme is apparently not mandatory (at least one concert has been held there).

The River Lambourn in springtime

or duck under the wire and walk on the grass at the edge of the gallops. Whatever the decision, make sure to head for the far left corner of the field.

10 At the corner of the field, go left to reach a footpath sign and from there head downhill. Do not go towards the barn; instead veer diagonally left towards a spot where

the track cum road down below takes a right turn.

11 It remains to go up the road and down the other side to where Manor Farm and the church and your car are to be found. Look out for the River Lambourn over in the corner of the bend. In April, when this walk was done, it was quite full of itself.

4 Hackpen Hill and Letcombe Bassett

Scenery of outstanding beauty embraced with multi-faceted history in this 5-mile walk

This is a transcendental walk, with its unspoilt natural beauty and more history in the little village of Letcombe Bassett than you can shake a stick at. Starting at Hackpen Hill, just off the Ridgeway, the trail skirts a magnificent cup or bowl feature before dropping down to the valley floor and the village of Letcombe Bassett. There a cottage that Thomas Hardy drew on for *Jude the Obscure* is inspected followed by an excursion to the fine little parish

Level: 🐾 🐾

Length: 5 miles

Terrain: One short steep-ish descent on a narrow grassy path and two minor ascents.

Park and start: The junction of the Ridgeway with the B4000 (GR 273843)

Map: OS Explorer 170

Websites: portal.oxfordshire.gov.uk/content/publicnet/council_services/environment_planning/countryside/countryside_access/mapping/HackpenHill

www.victorianweb.org/photos/hardy/50

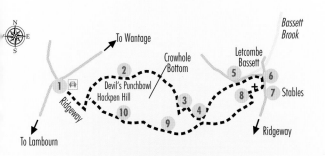

church where the restoration efforts of a famous Victorian architect are liable to be erased soon. The return route skirts the bowl but on the other side. Being consistently higher and longer it is perhaps more satisfying on that count.

Hackpen Hill and Letcombe Bassett

23

1 Walk eastwards along the Ridgeway until an old gate comes up on the left. Cross over a field to a modern gate. The display board announces that this is Hackpen Hill. Being open access there are several trails to be seen. Opt for the highest trail by a fence and proceed along the rim of the bowl, admiring the views. Letcombe Bassett can be seen down in the valley. Below to the

right is the feature known as the Devil's Punch Bowl, although the much larger Crowhole Bottom further over is perhaps more deserving of the epithet.

2 Continue skirting the bowl until, at some disused pits, curve right towards a stand of trees. Very soon start looking for a path down. A visual clue is another of the gates some way down the hill. Follow a narrow grassy

track down taking care not to twist an ankle (there are rabbits hereabouts).

3 Pass through the gate and turn left up a slope to reach a wide stretch of green sward bordering a field. Walk down to the bottom to meet a track running at right angles. According to the map a farm called Warren Farm East ought to be here or hereabouts but there is no sign — only some ruins.

4 In fact, the only building close by is a pumping station. Go left for a few yards and then right uphill, not stopping at the first junction but carrying on to another junction where the obvious move is to go left and continue past the pumping station to join a road into Letcombe Bassett.

The story attached to the better-known Devil's Punchbowl at Hindhead in Surrey may as well apply here. Legend has it that the devil spent his time tormenting the god Thor by pelting him with enormous handfuls of earth, leaving the bowl that can be seen today. Perhaps the devil got bored at this place because in truth the feature is no more than what one commentator called a 'scoop'. But Devil's Scoop doesn't quite cut it, does it?

The old name for Letcombe Bassett was Upper Letcombe. Perhaps it was an alternative name because the name "Bassett" was added as early as 1158 from the name of Richard Basset, who then owned the manor. Thomas Hardy called the village Cresscombe in his last and most controversial novel Jude the Obscure (see Fawleys walk).

(5) Turn right towards the centre of the village. Just before a gentrified Wesleyan chapel on the left is a thatched cottage set at the bottom of a steep flight of stairs and standing among the watercress beds. This cottage — Arabella's Cottage — was the model for the description of the home of Arabella Don in Hardy's novel, where she and Jude first met. After the last war these old cottages were apparently under threat but John Betjeman took a hand and the threat was averted. Had they been demolished, the village might have gone to the wall given the depleted number of inhabitants at this time.

6 Up from the centre of the village and opposite the road to the church is a racing stable but it was once the Rectory where the satirist and author of *Gulliver's Travels*, Dean Jonathan Swift, holed up in the period around 1714 before his exile to Ireland.

7 Walk up to the parish church St Michael and All Angels (called interestingly 'Downs Church' on the signpost).

8 To complete the walk go to the end of the church road and

turn left up a grassy track which bends right at the top. Continue through a gate and past another. The Ridgeway is just above you. Is Warren Farm East down below? No, it is not. Since, a little further on, Warren Farm West

Bassett Brook is the stream that feeds the local watercress beds, which were once famous. Once the railway arrived Bassett Cress was sent up to Covent Garden (where it would have competed with Cleve Cress from Blewbury, see the Blewbury walk).

The chancel and nave are 12th century; the tower 13th century. In the 19th century much of the interior was restored by William Butterfield, the architect who built Keble College, Oxford and also worked on the village hall. Butterfield's work having attracted some antipathy in the congregation, funds are being raised to reverse at least some of his work.

Looking back to the west

also fails to materialise, perhaps the mapmakers should insert '(remains of)' after the names of the farms.

9 Take the track branching off uphill but just before the top veer right and continue towards the

transmitter in the near distance. This section of the walk is particularly attractive. It is certainly the place for red kites. There is a rabbit crouching in the grass. Can red kites take on adult rabbits? Apparently it is a moot question.

10 At a gate head up across the grass to gain the high ground. Enjoy a last look down at Letcombe Bassett and Crowhole Bottom before reaching the entrance to Hackpen Hill from where it remains to cross the field to reach the Ridgeway and regain the car.

Looking back to Letcombe Bassett

5 **Farnborough**

A 6-mile ramble from Berkshire's highest village, where Betjeman once lived, to the Ridgeway and back

Level: 🥾
Length: 6 miles
Terrain: Bridleways, field tracks, two short sections of road
Park and start: At Farnborough church (GR 436819)
Map: OS Explorer 170
Websites: www.telegraph.co.uk/news/uknews/2963125/Sir-John-Betjemans-former-home-voted-Britains-best-parsonage-by-Country-Life

At 218 metres Farnborough is the highest village in Berkshire. It has strong associations with Sir John Betjeman who lived at the Rectory immediately after the last war. Heading east out of the village the route soon picks up an ancient track which takes it up to the Ridgeway. With splendid views north over the Vale of the White Horse the walk passes a monument to a soldier who won the first VC of the Crimean War, and later did much else. Tracks through woods and fields bring the walk back to Farnborough.

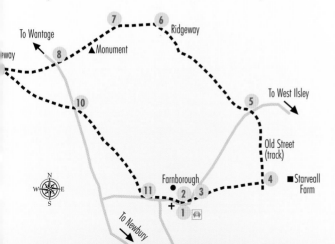

1 Like all downland churches All Saints' Church is satisfying in its own right but it has a special feature. To the left of the church door, in the chancel, is a stained glass window designed by John Piper in memory of his friend Sir John Betjeman.

2 Take the road south away from the village. After just a few yards the Old Rectory comes up on the left. This was once Betjeman's home; it is so well kept that no wonder it was voted Britain's best parsonage.

In 1945 the Old Rectory was bought from the church by Lord Chetwode as a very late wedding present for his daughter and son-in-law, Penelope and John Betjeman. When the family moved to Farnborough the house had no electricity or running water. Betjeman described it as 'dirty; but classy looking outside'. When they left in 1951 Penelope's comments suggest that the facilities indoors had barely improved.

The Piper window

3 Where the road bends fork right to go left of a farmyard. Pass by the water tower and proceed across a field. After the first hedge fine views open up to the east. Continue eastwards until reaching a track. This is Old Street or Old Street Lane, an ancient track that goes up to the Ridgeway.

This name Starveall is quite common in Berkshire and South Oxfordshire; at least two other farms with that name can be located. The name implies poor land, which begs the question of why anyone would buy such a place. Perhaps it was the thin chalk soil that gave rise to such foreboding. Whatever it was, farmers seem, as far as can be judged, to have scotched such fears.

4 Turn left and almost immediately notice a footpath off to the right. Don't take it however. It goes past Starveall Farm — an evocative sort of name.

5 After descending to a road, cross over and veer left past a house called Land's End to continue on Old Street which rises gradually until, with Wether Down to the left, the Ridgeway is reached.

6 The Ridgeway here is rather broad. When the original line became weathered or difficult to negotiate, travellers moved from one side to the other, gradually making the track wider. The way forward now is to the west by Ridgeway Down. Where the path forks take the left fork. Vying for attention with the marvellous views over the Vale of the White Horse to the north is a rather tall obelisk of some kind.

7 Where the track forks to skirt Betterton Down make a beeline for the monument cum memorial, for that is what it is. The steps on the monument would suit for lunch or a break. There are worse spots to linger.

8 Ahead is the car park by the B4494. Cross over the road and continue along the Ridgeway, as usual taking care. At 228 metres — one of the highest points on the Ridgeway — ignore

Monument to Lord Wantage

The monument is to Robert Loyd Lindsay, the first man to be awarded the VC in the Crimean War. He was one of the founders of the Red Cross and the memorial is located above the town from which he took his name when he became Lord Wantage in 1885. There is a story that the clumps of trees that stand in front of the monument were put there in imitation of the enemy troop emplacements Lindsay faced when he won the VC. Apocryphal? Maybe so, but it's a nice story.

the track cum road off to the left and continue over a rather unprepossessing section (considering what has been encountered so far) for half a mile or so before arriving at a junction with a track coming in from the left.

 Take this track and head south-eastwards over Lattin

Down past a house and through Triangle Wood before emerging again onto the B4494.

10 Enter the field opposite via a gate and head diagonally towards a point at the end of the hedge where a farm track comes up from Lockinge Kiln Farm (GR 423833).

Continue in the same direction rising towards Farnborough until reaching a house on the left from which a road can be seen.

11 Turn left at the road and follow it through the village before arriving at the church and the start of the walk.

View over the Vale of the White Horse

6 The Fawleys

An 8-mile circuit enjoying ever-changing views

This foray into the heart of the Downs brings ample rewards. There is a remote manor house with Popish plot connections, a strong association with Thomas Hardy, a touching monument, and a racing stable along with the ubiquitous gallops. The walk starts and finishes in the downland village of Brightwalton, known as Brickleton to its longer-standing inhabitants.

Level: 🥾 🥾
Length: 8½ miles
Terrain: Undulating, regularly reaching 200 metres; even so there are no great climbs.
Park and start: At Brightwalton village hall (GR 426793)
Map: OS Explorer 158 and 170
Websites: www.berkshirehistory.com/villages/fawley

www.users.globalnet.co.uk/~hadland/tvp/tvp12

A fine residence encountered en route

A338

9
11 10
▲ Memorial
12 13
14

rth ·ley

South ·awley To Wantage

Dogkennel Lane

To Hungerford

7 6
·atcombe ·bles

5
Manor Farm

4 3 2

1

🚌 ✚

● Brightwalton

Chaddleworth

N W E S

Chaddleworth was known for a curious legal custom. Any copyholder's widow who remarried forfeited her rights to her husband's lands. However, if she rode into court backwards on the back of a large black ram repeating certain ludicrous lines that end in a petition to give back her lands, the manor steward would be obliged to return them. Pure Monty Python.

 Turn right out of the village hall and go past the war memorial. Very soon a signpost to the right points across a large cornfield where in summer the way ahead will be unmistakeable.

2 Skirt the wood until a bend in a road comes up. Continue down this road for 300 metres or so before veering off right.

3 At a junction of tracks continue forwards along a narrow tree-hung path and go through a gate to enter a wide expanse of field. The fine house over to the right is Chaddleworth House (built 1809).

Cross in front of the house to a gate letting on to a road. Fifty yards up on the right is St Andrew's Church. Go through the churchyard and out the other side, stopping to inspect the church if the mood takes.

Rolling downlands near Fawley

The Fawleys

6

(4) Follow the track left for a short distance until a track across a field becomes apparent. Pause to admire the downland views. Cross the field, emerging onto a road. Follow the road down until it bends right. Take the track to the left.

(5) At Manor Farm cross the road before heading up the slope. Go over to a stile to the right of a gate. The buildings in view at the bottom are the Whatcombe stables. In the corner of the field hop over a double-barred stile and then pass to the left of another. Almost immediately go over another stile before proceeding downhill. Halfway down the field is another stile and at the bottom is a gate. Take care crossing the road for it is apt to be busy.

37

6 A short distance up the minor road opposite is the entrance to the stables. Pass through a gate and walk towards the house. Just before the house go right and look for a path northwards through a narrow avenue of trees, somewhat overgrown, before emerging into an open space with a field to the left.

South Fawley Manor was built in 1614 for Sir Francis Moore, MP for Reading and a well-connected lawyer who, seems to have had Catholic sympathies. It was said, for instance, that he could have prevented the Gunpowder Plot. Royalist troops quartered themselves in the house for one night in 1644, during the Civil War. The track just followed may well have been that used by Catholic sympathisers – conspirators even – housed at Whatcombe and South Fawley Manor.

7 Continue upwards, skirting another field, until reaching a stile to the right. After two more stiles exit onto the road. The fine house over to the right is South Fawley Manor.

8 South Fawley consists of but a few houses and some farm buildings. Across the road is a bench that offers the chance of a breather.

South Fawley Manor

The bench bears the inscription 'to Ken who loved life and people and sheep'. Beyond the farmyard is a choice of routes: take the track off at half right. After 15 minutes or so North Fawley comes up.

(9) Proceed through Fawley and down the road to the A338. Take extreme care crossing.

(10) There is a monument — a cross — off to the right. It is a memorial to a scion of the Wroughton family who was killed in the Great War. The Wroughtons continue to reside in nearby Woolley Park. To inspect it is necessary to approach via the road. Otherwise go over the stile and then through a squeeze stile. From there skirt the gallops and

North Fawley or Great Fawley or just Fawley is associated with Thomas Hardy and his last and most controversial novel Jude the Obscure *(he ceased writing novels after the opprobrium it attracted). Hardy has Jude growing up in 'Marygreen', as he called it, although it has been suggested that Lambourn is the real life location. But Hardy did call Jude 'Jude Fawley'.*

Looking back to the avenue of horse chestnuts

planted horse chestnut trees. While strolling down the avenue take in the fine views across to the North Hampshire Downs.

13 At a road junction pause to admire the house at the side. The way ahead across a field is clearly marked. Proceed to the edge of the wood.

14 Enter the wood briefly before exiting south-eastwards towards another wood, and then, after skirting that, carry on until a road is reached (Common Lane). From there it is but a few hundred yards back to the start.

proceed in a parallel fashion to the minor road until reaching the road (GR 403806). Once there turn north-east towards Woolley Down Cottages.

11 Go up Woolley Down staying close to the gallops. At a T-junction take the bridleway to the right and continue for almost a mile. At some point look back to the south-west to view South Fawley Manor, which before seemed quite tucked away. What wide-ranging views it has to the north and the east! Ideal for keeping a lookout.

12 At the top of the slope take the direction indicated by the signpost. Quite soon join a pleasant strip of farm road bordered by recently

7 East Ilsley

A 5-mile circuit that showcases what downland walking is all about

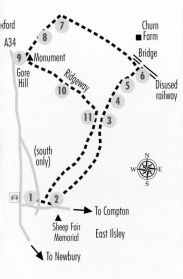

Level:
Length: 5 miles
Terrain: Up and down but nothing steep; mostly chalk tracks, one lovely stretch of sward.
Park and start: Abingdon Lane, East Ilsley; just by the Sheepdown cul-de-sac (GR 493813).
Map: OS Explorer 170
Websites:
www.east.ilsley.btinternet.co.uk/fairs

Here is quintessential downland walking that goes up to the Ridgeway, dives down to a long disused railway, climbs back up again to the Ridgeway, passes a memorial — yes, another memorial on the Downs — before dropping down again to the start, all the while offering gorgeous views. After finishing it is well worth taking a look at the village. This was a sheep fair village, perhaps the sheep fair village. The fair began in the reign of Henry III and continued until 1934. Sheep pens permanently lined the High Street, Broad Street and Pen Meadow which was the actual site of the fair. Go up beyond the Crown and Horns (someone racked their brains for this sheepish take) to see a commemorative plaque and a 1776 milestone.

Looking back to East Ilsley

1 Cross the road and follow the footpath between the houses. At a four-way junction carry on to reach a road.

2 Turn left past Summer Down stables and proceed up the bridleway towards the downs. Immediately to the left is a single file gallop which soon widens into a double and then into gallops proper

when the track starts to curve to the left just before it reaches the Ridgeway.

3 On the Ridgeway don't worry about the absence of a signpost but press on over some fine sward. Spread out if you are in numbers but make sure to take in the fine views to the north and the east that are opening up.

4 Beyond the next gate Churn Farm can be seen below, and above it Churn Hill. In front of Churn Farm there was a railway, the only railway to cross the Downs. This railway – the Didcot, Newbury and Southampton Junction Railway – was nicknamed the "Desert line" because it ran through largely unpopulated farming districts. Not a problem then for Dr Beeching.

5 Go downhill past Fox Barrow and turn right at a footpath sign before curving left to arrive at an old railway bridge. There was a station here or hereabouts – Churn Halt. It is about 200 yards down the line to the right.

Churn Halt was a small and very isolated single platform halt with access only via an unmetalled downland sheep road. It was built as a temporary stop to accommodate a competition held by the National Rifle Association in 1888. However, from 1889 military summer camps were established near to the station which required the use of the halt as the only access to the site. For trains to call at Churn prior notice had to be given to the Stationmaster at Didcot (difficult in the early days without telephones).

Looking down on Churn Farm and the bed of the disused railway

6 Return from the bridge for a few yards and go right to join the old track bed. Follow it for a while, enjoying that regular comfortable feel that comes from walking a disused railway. The track bed starts to curve to the right before arriving at a crossing of the ways.

The A34 road crosses the Ridgeway at Gore Hill. It has been a notorious spot for travellers for many years. In 1830 the Southampton coach from Oxford "was enclosed so fast in snow at Gore Hill the coachman and passenger were necessitated to leave it". 150 years later, the snows of the winter of 1981/2 also caused people to abandon their vehicles for the warmth and comfort of the pubs and schoolrooms of East Ilsley.

The Grosvenor memorial

7 Turn left in the direction of the Ridgeway. The transmitter up ahead is situated on Gore Hill.

8 At a junction there is a choice of track ahead – narrow or broad. Take the broad track to the right of the hedge which will join the narrow track at the top. Proceed through some woods until the track levels before arriving at the transmitter. Go left to join the Ridgeway again.

9 Very soon on the left look out for a smallish brown stone erected to the memory of Hugh Grosvenor, a Life Guard, who died in an armoured car accident in April 1947, aged 19. Surely the accident wasn't here on the Ridgeway? It must have been on the A34. The memorial says only that the young soldier died near the spot.

10 Over to the right is Sheep Down, not a sheep to be seen when this walk was done. To the left in the middle distance are the iconic Wittenham Clumps. Further along on the right, opposite Several Down, was situated, although you could not guess it, the East Ilsley racecourse, a figure-of-eight construction with one loop in the area in view and the other loop on the

Sheep Fair plaque

right hand side of the bridleway that constituted the first part of the walk. The racecourse was still in existence in 1850.

11 The last leg of the route soon comes up. At a break in the gallops railings cross over the gallops and proceed down into East Ilsley. At the four-way junction met at the start of the walk go right and back down to the car.

1776 milestone

8 **Blewbury**

Two parts to this 3-mile walk really: the downland and the village with artistic associations

Mill Brook

Blewbury

Churn
Knob

H ere is a walk that climbs from the charming village of Blewbury (old name Blewberry) to visit an iconic ecclesiastical feature on the Downs and to drink in the views. Back in Blewbury there is the chance to explore the village including the houses once occupied by Kenneth Grahame, author of *Wind in the Willows*, and Sir William Nicholson the painter, father of Ben. Another author who lived in the village was Barbara Euphan Todd, creator of *Worzel Gummidge*.

Level:

Length: 3½ miles (assuming half a mile meandering around Blewbury)

Terrain: Single climb up, descent down, some village walking

Park and start: On Westbrook Street just off the A417 (GR 527856)

Map: OS Explorer 170

Websites: www.stbirinuspilgrimage.org.uk/StBPilg%20infolflt-web.pdf
www.bbc.co.uk/dna/h2g2/A26179239
www.online-literature.com/grahame
www.geograph.org.uk/sitemap/SU/48/6/SU5284

Nicholson House

Looking over Blewbury

1 Across the A417 is a signed footpath. Take it and almost immediately come to a house with a plaque attached. The inscription says that Marguerite Steen, the novelist, lived here with perhaps the rather better known artist William Nicholson from 1943 until his death in 1949. After a short wooded section keep climbing gently until a wide track that is obviously driven over is reached.

2 Ahead and over to the left is the tumulus called Churn Knob, also known as St Birinus' Mound. There was a large wooden cross to the side but it has fallen or been taken down (a 2006 image can be found on the Geograph website). Perhaps the devil tired of chucking stones (Hackpen Hill walk) and came along here in search of further mischief.

It was upon this mound that the Saint Birinus was supposed to have met King Cynegils of Wessex in AD 634. The King must have reckoned this ancient pagan place to be a fine spot to intimidate the newcomer. However, Birinus was seemingly unperturbed and even – it is said – managed to convert the King to Christianity. Every year in June there is a pilgrimage from Churn Knob to Dorchester-on-Thames.

Churn Knob

3 To get up close to Churn Knob go left and then when the track starts to veer right go more sharply right towards a clump of trees that caps Churn Hill. Skirt the trees and make for the south side of Churn Knob. Lying there half-hidden by undergrowth, the cross is a sad sight. The parish people hope to have it re-erected before the next pilgrimage.

(4) To the left of the tumulus looking north is a familiar sight to many — Didcot Power Station. Go back along the track admiring the views to the north. The feature called Wittenham Clumps is prominent. Back at the junction for Churn Knob go right and proceed southwards past a dwelling to the left (Upper Chance Farm).

(5) When a track to the left comes up take it and skirt the farmhouse. Continue onwards, first

bearing right and then left, all the while enjoying downland views second to none, until a major track is reached. This is a continuation of a little road called Woodway.

(6) Go left to join the road and carry on down it for a short distance until a footpath sign comes

In 2003 Country Life readers voted Didcot Power Station Britain's third worst eyesore but it has won architectural awards for how well it blends into the landscape.

A Blewbury cottage

The Mill Brook

Blewbury Mill has a claim to fame. It is said (by some) to be the place where blotting paper was invented, albeit and inevitably accidentally. It will come as no surprise to learn that a rival account places the invention in Norfolk at Lyng Mill on the River Wensum. No doubt there are other claimants. For the record, blotting paper is first mentioned in the year 1465.

up on the left. Take this track back to Blewbury. On reaching the main road after the descent (opposite the *Barley Mow* pub) cross the road left towards a little green space with low wooden benches.

 The space is called The Pound. Conveniently there is a display board mapping out Blewbury and the sights to be seen. Do what takes your fancy. As a suggestion why not set off on the path to the left of the board towards the Methodist Chapel? Once there continue down past a house called 'The Cleve' to reach a stretch of water, the Cleve itself, from where once upon a time watercress was sent daily to London.

8 Continue on to another green space, a triangular space, called the Playclose. Those walls with the lengths of thatch on top are called 'cob walls' and were once a common feature of villages hereabouts. At the edge of the Playclose is a pretty

stream, the Mill Brook, which rises from springs in the village and enters the Thames at Wallingford. The Old Mill on the northern outskirts of the village is now a private residence. It is not to be confused with Blewbury Mill, further north, where there is however very little left to see.

(9) Keep going westwards from the Playclose to reach the northern end of Westbrook Street, close to Bohams, a Tudor farmhouse. This was Kenneth Grahame's house. It remains to walk down Westbrook Street to the start, taking in the picturesque cottages on the left.

Grahame and his family lived at Bohams from 1910 to 1924. At the age of 41 when he already had a family there was a new arrival, Alastair. Nicknamed 'Mouse', the boy seems to have endured a troubled existence (as anyone might with such a nickname). On 7 May 1920 he was found dead by railway tracks near Oxford.

Cottages in Westbrook Street

9 **Streatley**

Strangely, <u>down</u> to the Ridgeway then up in a 6-mile circuit that will have the lungs going

Level: 🥾 🥾 🥾
Length: 6 miles
Terrain: Moderate / Strenuous
Park and start: At the National Trust car park off the B4009 (GR 583806)
Map: OS Explorer 170, 159

H istorically situated in Berkshire, Streatley almost certainly derives from 'street' referring to the Roman road from Silchester to Dorchester-on-Thames that went through it.

It was Mark Twain who remarked that "Golf is a good walk spoilt". Funny how walkers and golfers go together; golf course designers by and large seek out the best, most mind-blowing terrain — just as walkers do. Actually, walkers and golfers don't really go together — both would prefer to avoid the other although of course some double up. At any rate this walk steers clear of the golf course. It starts by passing through two quite superb NT areas en route to the Ridgeway — Lardon Chase, an SSSI with butterflies the special feature, and its neighbour Lough Down — and it finishes in another NT area, across the road from the car park, the Holies. In between, the walk climbs back from the Ridgeway to the B4009 before heading south-east and then east to skirt a series of fields before, just prior to reaching the Holies, walking a section of Grim's Ditch, thought by medieval folk to be the work of the devil.

[Map showing: Thurle Grange, Sarsen Stone, Golf Club, Streatley, Goring, A417, A329, River Thames, Kiddington Cottage, The Holies, Wood Farm Stables, Grim's Ditch, Gould's Cottage, with numbered points 1-13]

1 Go through the gate into Lardon Chase. The views over to the Chilterns and, down below, Goring and the Thames, might just take your breath away. There are benches along the way to allow for reflection.

View over Goring and the Thames

2 Look out for a gate over to the left that lets into Lough Down. Follow an obvious path through the grass and descend to the Ridgeway, as it happens. The last section of the descent is quite steep. Go through a gate near to the bottom and out onto the Ridgeway.

3 It feels odd to say this is the Ridgeway. Not only is it a road with a fair bit of traffic (blame the golf club for that); it is also quite built up. And it is strange to be *descending* to the Ridgeway where everywhere else has required an ascent. Of course there

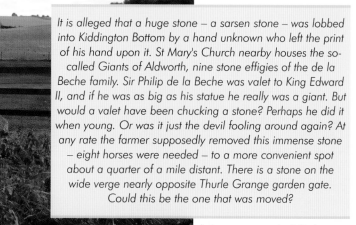

It is alleged that a huge stone – a sarsen stone – was lobbed into Kiddington Bottom by a hand unknown who left the print of his hand upon it. St Mary's Church nearby houses the so-called Giants of Aldworth, nine stone effigies of the de la Beche family. Sir Philip de la Beche was valet to King Edward II, and if he was as big as his statue he really was a giant. But would a valet have been chucking a stone? Perhaps he did it when young. Or was it just the devil fooling around again? At any rate the farmer supposedly removed this immense stone – eight horses were needed – to a more convenient spot about a quarter of a mile distant. There is a stone on the wide verge nearly opposite Thurle Grange garden gate. Could this be the one that was moved?

Sarsen stone or what? Can't you see the palm print?

is a good reason for that – the Thames. Walk left down the road soon passing the clubhouse and continue along the road until a property called

Thurle Grange is reached. Note the fine topiary. But what is that sitting in the grass opposite? Just up the road on the left is a signpost by a house.

(4) Take the path which looks like an old green lane until a field comes up on the right. Carry on straight ahead through some woodland until meeting the field

again. Head left towards a building that has come into view. This area is Kiddington Bottom and the extremely isolated dwelling is Kiddington Cottage, formerly Kiddington Farm.

5 Continue past Kiddington Cottage to join a partly made-up track that serves as an access road for the cottage. This track has been the source of some dispute. Several times the owners have petitioned for a new surface to facilitate driving but each time they have been turned down.

6 Eventually the track levels out and passes some farm buildings. At the B4009 turn left for 150 yards or so before turning right down a little road that leads to

Pheasants on the road near Gould's Cottage

The latest judgement stresses that this is a public footpath. "The site is located in open countryside within the North Wessex Downs Area of Outstanding Natural Beauty. The proposed surface would result in a highly conspicuous and inappropriate urbanising visual feature, which would have a detrimental impact on the character of this attractive and open area of countryside." It's not a sentiment voiced that often but let's hear it for the planners!

another very isolated cottage, Gould's Cottage, another cottage that was once a farm. Once there do not carry straight on as the marked footpath on the map would indicate but instead turn left.

(7) Follow a series of grassy tracks along the edges of several fields to go under overhead

power lines to reach what is evidently the boundary of a garden. Go left and pass the house to which the garden belongs – Wood Farm Stables.

(8) At the road turn right and continue round a bend until another road comes in on the right. At this junction there is a designation

Holies Shaw ('shaw' means a thicket or small wood or copse) and a footpath sign pointing up a road, marked on the map as Grim's Ditch.

The reference is to earthworks probably dating back to the Bronze Age. It appears all over the Chilterns and Berkshire Downs. 'Grim' was the Saxon word for the devil and the Saxons thought these features were so large that only the devil could have constructed them. It seems that they were built to demarcate territory; in this case, between the Berkshire Downs and the Vale of the White Horse.

Wood Farm Stables courtyard

Looking south over the Holies

Red Arrows

woodland to reach the A329 and a car park. Pass through a quite challenging gate and enter the Holies.

(11) Follow an obvious grass track curving round to the right before reaching a gate. Relish the fine views over to the Chilterns. From the gate go up the partly metalled track. Look back and there are fine views to the south.

(12) Pass through a gate into Common Wood and bear left to arrive at some open common land. Expect wonderful tree colours in autumn.

(13) It remains to go down and then up and along some flat to arrive back at the B4009 and the car park.

(9) Grim's Ditch continues for half a mile or so. The ditch builders would not have been bothered by Red Arrows but here they were — screaming overhead, giving the writer a jolt as well as patently alarming some sheep.

(10) At the top of the incline carry on down through some

10 Moulsford

A 7-mile circuit that offers sundry pleasures, from Thames to Roman temple remains

Think of Moulsford and what comes to mind? It must be the Beetle and Wedge. Followed very closely perhaps by *Three Men in a Boat* and images of Griff Rhys-Jones and his pals messing about on the river? But this walk is not about the Thames. It is about heading into the hills. After a gradual ascent to the Ridgeway the walk comes close to the site of a

Roman temple and to another section of Grim's Ditch. Side trips are possible before returning along the feature called the Fair Mile. Back in Moulsford perhaps it is time to visit the church — small,

Level: 🦋 🦋
Length: 7¾ miles
Terrain: Only one climb to speak of; ground good under foot although with its multiple ruts the Fair Mile could be challenging.
Park and start: In the village in a car park beside the telephone box (GR 591838)
Map: OS Explorer 170
Websites: www.themodernantiquarian.com/site/9401/lowbury_hill_camp
bdb.co.za/shackle/articles/beetle.htm

tucked away and exquisite in its contours — before seeking out refreshment at the Beetle and Wedge. A beetle by the way is a heavy hammer used to split logs; a wedge is a wedge. The signs to the restaurant display an appropriate image.

1 The car park lies next to the A329, called by the locals 'The Street' (as with Streatley the reference is to the Roman road). Before departing look across The Street to the Clock House, formerly the village school room which was open from 1851 to 1972. Then about turn and cross the excellent recreation ground towards a play area featuring a slide and a climbing frame. On the other side go left to reach a field.

2 Proceed up the field until directed left to enter another field. Go up this field to a road (the A417). Opposite, and take care when crossing, is the well-guarded entrance to Well Barn Estate and more particularly to Starveall Farm – yes, another Starveall Farm (see Farnborough walk).

3 Pass through a gate and walk up towards the farm. The hill to the right has some claim to fame.

4 Go through a gate and skirt the farm. At a signpost and bend in the road enter the field opposite and proceed along a dry valley or 'bottom' (it becomes Unhill Bottom).

Kingstanding Hill (King's Standing Hill) may have been the site of the last great battle between the invading Danes and King Alfred or – more likely – a place where the Saxons re-grouped after their failure to drive the Danes out of Reading. The showdown then took place further west at the Battle of Ashdown (Ashdown walk).

(5) Pass through a gap in the hedge where a pump station is marked on the map but of which there is no trace. Continue along a more clearly defined track bearing right past a tree and up towards the corner of some woodland. There join some tarmac.

(6) Follow the signpost up the tarmac and continue to the end of the tarmac turning to admire the views back to the Chilterns and also to the north where our old friend Didcot Power Station materialises.

(7) Beyond the tarmac is a stretch of green sward. Carry on to the top.

(8) Continue through some woodland until a dwelling comes up on the left. Hop over a stile and join the road that serves the house. Follow the road to a gate and exit Well Barn Estate to join the Ridgeway.

(9) Passing Warren Farm to the right, noting that there is yet another Starveall Farm off to the left,

Starveall Farm from Kingstanding Hill

Looking back to the Chilterns

look for a footpath off to the right. When it comes up follow a path to the left of a hedge. Beyond the hedge continue on a headland admiring the views to the west which are opening out.

(10) Over to the left are the remains of Lowbury Hill Roman temple. In truth there is nothing much to see. The comments of a blogger - "the last time I went up to Lowbury, there was def (sic) some bumps of round barrows there; if they are Bronze Age or Roman, I do not know" about sums it up. There is however a memorial on the trig point. The views all around are marvellous. As usual, the Romans chose well.

(11) Go down the incline to reach a junction of tracks. A little way further down a section of Grim's Ditch is marked on the map. Busy hereabouts, that devil, but then time has hardly been a limiting factor. But without Grim Ditcher eyes the writer could not discern the Ditch.

(12) Back at the junction turn to the east and continue straight until the multiple ruts of the Fair Mile become evident. Carry on down the Fair Mile until a metalled by-way is reached.

> *The Fair Mile was obviously a main thoroughfare of choice for carts and coaches which could pass side by side. In 1743 it was defined to be 132 feet wide. Nothing much else seems to be known about it.*

13 Proceed down the by-way for three-quarters of a mile to reach the A417.

14 Taking great care cross over to Halfpenny Lane which is signed to Moulsford.

15 After about 300 yards there is a footpath off to the right.

Take this ancient-feeling track all the way down to the outskirts of Moulsford.

16 Go right past the school and follow the road along to a sports field. Take an obvious diagonal path across the field to arrive once again at the children's play area. From there cross the recreation ground back to the car.